M

by Iain Gray

WRITING *to* REMEMBER

PUBLISHING

WRITING *to* REMEMBER

79 Main Street, Newtongrange,
Midlothian EH22 4NA
Tel: 0131 344 0414
E-mail: info@lang-syne.co.uk
www.langsyneshop.co.uk

Design by Dorothy Meikle
Printed by Printwell Ltd
© Lang Syne Publishers Ltd 2022

All rights reserved. No part of this publication may be reproduced, stored or introduced into a retrieval system, or transmitted in any form or by any means (electronic, mechanical, photocopying, recording or otherwise) without the prior written permission of Lang Syne Publishers Ltd.

ISBN 978-1-85217-535-1

Morris

MOTTO:
If God be with us, who can be against us
(and)
The word of God above all.

CREST:
A lion rampant.

NAME variations include:
  Moris
  Moriss
  Morrice
  Morriss

Chapter one:

The origins of popular surnames

by George Forbes and Iain Gray

***If you don't know where you came from, you won't know where you're going* is a frequently quoted observation and one that has a particular resonance today when there has been a marked upsurge in interest in genealogy, with increasing numbers of people curious to trace their family roots.**

Main sources for genealogical research include census returns and official records of births, marriages and deaths – and the key to unlocking the detail they contain is obviously a family surname, one that has been 'inherited' and passed from generation to generation.

No matter our station in life, we all have a surname – but it was not until about the middle of the fourteenth century that the practice of being identified by a particular surname became commonly established throughout the British Isles.

Previous to this, it was normal for a person to be identified through the use of only a forename.

But as population gradually increased and there were many more people with the same forename, surnames were adopted to distinguish one person, or community, from another.

Many common English surnames are patronymic in origin, meaning they stem from the forename of one's father – with 'Johnson,' for example, indicating 'son of John.'

It was the Normans, in the wake of their eleventh century conquest of Anglo-Saxon England, a pivotal moment in the nation's history, who first brought surnames into usage – although it was a gradual process.

For the Normans, these were names initially based on the title of their estates, local villages and chateaux in France to distinguish and identify these landholdings.

Such grand descriptions also helped enhance the prestige of these warlords and generally glorify their lofty positions high above the humble serfs slaving away below in the pecking order who had only single names, often with Biblical connotations as in Pierre and Jacques.

The only descriptive distinctions among the peasantry concerned their occupations, like 'Pierre the swineherd' or 'Jacques the ferryman.'

Roots of surnames that came into usage in England not only included Norman-French, but also Old French, Old Norse, Old English, Middle English, German, Latin, Greek, Hebrew and the Gaelic languages of the Celts.

The Normans themselves were originally Vikings, or 'Northmen', who raided, colonised and eventually settled down around the French coastline.

They had sailed up the Seine in their longboats in 900AD under their ferocious leader Rollo and ruled the roost in north eastern France before sailing over to conquer England in 1066 under Duke William of Normandy – better known to posterity as William the Conqueror, or King William I of England.

Granted lands in the newly-conquered England, some of their descendants later acquired territories in Wales, Scotland and Ireland – taking not only their own surnames, but also the practice of adopting a surname, with them.

But it was in England where Norman rule and custom first impacted, particularly in relation to the adoption of surnames.

This is reflected in the famous *Domesday Book*, a massive survey of much of England and Wales, ordered by William I, to determine who owned what, what it was worth and therefore how much they were liable to pay in taxes to the voracious Royal Exchequer.

Completed in 1086 and now held in the National Archives in Kew, London, 'Domesday' was an Old English word meaning 'Day of Judgement.'

This was because, in the words of one contemporary chronicler, "its decisions, like those of the Last Judgement, are unalterable."

It had been a requirement of all those English landholders – from the richest to the poorest – that they identify themselves for the purposes of the survey and for future reference by means of a surname.

This is why the *Domesday Book*, although written in Latin as was the practice for several centuries with both civic and ecclesiastical records, is an invaluable source for the early appearance of a wide range of English surnames.

Several of these names were coined in connection with occupations.

These include Baker and Smith, while Cooks, Chamberlains, Constables and Porters were to be found carrying out duties in large medieval households.

The church's influence can be found in names such as Bishop, Friar and Monk while the popular name of Bennett derives from the late fifth to mid-sixth century Saint Benedict, founder of the Benedictine order of monks.

The early medical profession is represented by Barber, while businessmen produced names that include Merchant and Sellers.

Down at the village watermill, the names that cropped up included Millar/Miller, Walker and Fuller, while other self-explanatory trades included Cooper, Tailor, Mason and Wright.

Even the scenery was utilised as in Moor, Hill, Wood and Forrest – while the hunt and the chase supplied names that include Hunter, Falconer, Fowler and Fox.

Colours are also a source of popular surnames, as in Black, Brown, Gray/Grey, Green and White, and would have denoted the colour of the clothing the person habitually wore or, apart from the obvious exception of 'Green', one's hair colouring or even complexion.

The surname Red developed into Reid, while

Blue was rare and no-one wanted to be associated with yellow.

Rather self-important individuals took surnames that include Goodman and Wiseman, while physical attributes crept into surnames such as Small and Little.

Many families proudly boast the heraldic device known as a Coat of Arms, as featured on our front cover.

The central motif of the Coat of Arms would originally have been what was borne on the shield of a warrior to distinguish himself from others on the battlefield.

Not featured on the Coat of Arms, but highlighted on page three, is the family motto and related crest – with the latter frequently different from the central motif.

Adding further variety to the rich cultural heritage that is represented by surnames is the appearance in recent times in lists of the 100 most common names found in England of ones that include Khan, Patel and Singh – names that have proud roots in the vast sub-continent of India.

Echoes of a far distant past can still be found in our surnames and they can be borne with pride in commemoration of our forebears.

Chapter two:

Invasion and conquest

Ranked at 34th in some lists of the 100 most common surnames in England, 'Morris' has a number of points of origin that include the Old Welsh 'Morris', derived in turn from the Latin personal name 'Mauritius' and indicating a dark or swarthy person.

Another point of origin is from the place-name of St Maurice in Normandy and it would have been further popularised throughout the British Isles in the wake of the Norman Conquest of 1066.

But the roots of the name lay much further back in time, and this means that flowing through the veins of many of its bearers today is a rich and heady mixed brew of the blood of the ancient Britons, the Anglo-Saxons, Vikings and Normans.

Of Celtic pedigree, the original Britons were settled for centuries from a line south of the River Forth in Scotland all the way down to the south coast of England and with a particular presence in Wales.

Speaking a Celtic language known as Brythonic, they boasted a glorious culture that flourished even after the Roman invasion of Britain in 43 AD and the subsequent consolidation of Roman power by about 84 AD.

With many of the original Britons absorbing aspects of Roman culture, they became 'Romano-British' – while still retaining their own proud Celtic heritage.

Following the withdrawal of the last Roman legions from Britain in 406, what is now modern-day Wales, or *Cymru*, fragmented into a number of independent kingdoms – with the most powerful king being regarded as overall ruler.

Recognised as King of the Britons, he had to battle with not only internal rivals but also the depredations of the wild sea rovers known as the Vikings, or Northmen, and also the Anglo-Saxons – those Germanic tribes who invaded and settled in the south and east of the island of Britain from about the early fifth century.

They were composed of the Jutes, from the area of the Jutland Peninsula in modern Denmark, the Saxons from Lower Saxony, in modern Germany and the Angles from the Angeln area of Germany.

It was the Angles who gave the name 'Engla land', or 'Aengla land' – better known as 'England.'

They held sway from approximately 550 to 1066, with the main kingdoms those of Sussex, Wessex, Northumbria, Mercia, Kent, East Anglia and Essex.

Whoever controlled the most powerful of these kingdoms was tacitly recognised as overall 'king' – one of the most noted being Alfred the Great, King of Wessex from 871 to 899.

It was during his reign that the famous *Anglo-Saxon Chronicle* was compiled – an invaluable source of Anglo-Saxon history – while Alfred was designated in early documents as *Rex Anglorum Saxonum*, King of the English Saxons.

Other important Anglo-Saxon works include the epic *Beowulf* and the seventh century *Caedmon's Hymn*.

The Anglo-Saxons meanwhile, had usurped the power of the indigenous Britons such as those found in Wales and who would later come to bear the Morris name – and who referred to them as 'Saeson' or 'Saxones.'

It is from this that the Scottish Gaelic term for 'English people' of 'Sasannach' derives, the Irish Gaelic 'Sasanach' and the Welsh 'Saeson.'

We learn from the *Anglo-Saxon Chronicle*

how the religion of the early Anglo-Saxons was one that pre-dated the establishment of Christianity in the British Isles.

Known as a form of Germanic paganism, with roots in Old Norse religion, it shared much in common with the Druidic 'nature-worshipping' religion of the indigenous Britons.

It was in the closing years of the sixth century that Christianity began to take a hold in Britain, while by approximately 690 it had become the 'established' religion of Anglo-Saxon England.

The first serious shock to Anglo-Saxon control came in 789 in the form of sinister black-sailed Viking ships that appeared over the horizon off the island monastery of Lindisfarne, in the northeast of the country.

The monastery was sacked in an orgy of violence and plunder, setting the scene for what would be many more terrifying raids on the coastline of not only England, but also of Wales, Ireland and Scotland.

But the Vikings, or 'Northmen', in common with the Anglo-Saxons of earlier times, were raiders who eventually stayed – establishing, for example, what became Jorvik, or York, and the trading port of Dublin, in Ireland.

Through intermarriage, the bloodlines of the Anglo-Saxons also became infused with that of the Vikings.

But there would be another infusion of the blood of the 'Northmen' in the wake of the Norman Conquest of 1066 – a key event in English history that sounded the death knell of Anglo-Saxon supremacy.

By this date, England had become a nation with several powerful competitors to the throne.

In what were extremely complex family, political and military machinations, the king was Harold II, who had succeeded to the throne following the death of Edward the Confessor.

But his right to the throne was contested by two powerful competitors – his brother-in-law King Harold Hardrada of Norway, in alliance with Tostig, Harold II's brother, and Duke William II of Normandy.

In what has become known as The Year of Three Battles, Hardrada invaded England and gained victory over the English king on September 20 at the battle of Fulford, in Yorkshire.

Five days later, however, Harold II decisively defeated his brother-in-law and brother at the battle of Stamford Bridge.

But he had little time to celebrate his victory,

having to immediately march south from Yorkshire to encounter a mighty invasion force, led by Duke William of Normandy, that had landed at Hastings, in East Sussex.

Harold's battle-hardened but exhausted force confronted the Normans on October 14 in a battle subsequently depicted on the Bayeux tapestry – a 23ft. long strip of embroidered linen thought to have been commissioned eleven years after the event by the Norman Odo of Bayeux.

Harold drew up a strong defensive position at the top of Senlac Hill, building a shield wall to repel Duke William's cavalry and infantry.

The Normans suffered heavy losses, but through a combination of the deadly skill of their archers and the ferocious determination of their cavalry they eventually won the day.

Anglo-Saxon morale had collapsed on the battlefield as word spread through the ranks that Harold had been killed – the Bayeux Tapestry depicting this as having happened when he was struck by an arrow to the head.

Amidst the carnage of the battlefield, it was difficult to identify him – the last of the Anglo-Saxon kings.

Some sources assert William ordered his body to be thrown into the sea, while others state it was secretly buried at Waltham Abbey.

What is known with certainty, however, is that William in celebration of his great victory founded Battle Abbey, near the site of the battle, ordering that the altar be sited on the spot where Harold was believed to have fallen.

William was declared King of England on December 25, and the complete subjugation of his Anglo-Saxon subjects followed.

Those Normans who had fought on his behalf were rewarded with the lands of Anglo-Saxons, many of whom sought exile abroad as mercenaries.

Within an astonishingly short space of time, Norman manners, customs and law were imposed, laying the basis for what subsequently became established 'English' custom and practice.

In 1282, by which time most of Wales had come under Anglo-Norman rule, final rebellion against this was crushed by England's Edward I, and it is from this date that the heir apparent to the British throne has borne the title of Prince of Wales.

An abortive rebellion was led in the early fifteenth century by the freedom fighter Owain

Glyndŵr, while in the following century, under Henry VIII, Wales was 'incorporated' into the English kingdom; in 1707, in common with Scotland, Wales became part of the United Kingdom.

Flourishing not only in their original heartland of Wales, but also throughout the British Isles, bearers of the Morris name feature prominently in the historical record.

Chapter three:

Fame and infamy

On the high seas, one particularly infamous bearer of the Morris name was the English buccaneer John Morris whose date of birth has been lost to posterity.

With the acquiescence of the English government, he captained his own vessel under the overall command of the feared buccaneer and privateer Admiral Sir Henry Morgan in attacks against Spanish strongholds in the Caribbean.

This included the seizure of the Spanish-held islands of Providencia, Colombia and Santa Catalina, while in December of 1670 they captured the fortress of San Lorenzo on the coast of Panama and slaughtered 300 of its Spanish garrison.

With Morris leading the assault, Morgan and his band of ruthless pirates later captured the city of Panama itself.

Its inhabitants were tortured in a feverish search for gold, with Morgan and his blood-thirsty crew sacking the city to such an extent that it had to be completely rebuilt later on a new site several kilometres to the west. The sack of Panama had violated a peace treaty and Morgan was arrested and taken back to England to face the consequences.

But, claiming he had been unaware of the treaty, instead of being punished he was actually knighted and, fourteen years before his death in 1688, appointed to the powerful and lucrative post of Lieutenant Governor of Jamaica.

Morris, who had not been arrested, died in 1672 shortly after being given command of the frigate *Lily*.

He and Morgan have since been immortalised in a number of books and films, notably the 1935 *Captain Blood*, starring a swashbuckling Errol Flynn and adapted from a novel by Rafael Sabatini.

Also on the high seas, but of a decidedly more respectable character than John Morris, Vice-Admiral Sir James Morris was the Royal Navy officer who was noted by his contemporaries as having a strict sense of honour and "simplicity and singleness of heart for which he was remarkable."

Born into a seafaring family in Northamptonshire in 1763 and joining the Royal Navy when aged only twelve, he rose to serve with great distinction during the American War of Independence of 1775 to 1783, the French Revolutionary War and the Napoleonic Wars – most notably, under the overall command of Lord Horatio Nelson, at the battle of Trafalgar in October of 1805.

It was at the great naval battle of Trafalgar that, in command of HMS *Colossus*, Morris disabled a number of French vessels that included the *Swiftsure* and the *Bahama* before his vessel was shot through by two other French ships with the loss of 206 men killed or wounded – the highest casualty rate of any vessel in the fleet.

Morris was shot in the knee and later collapsed from loss of blood after refusing to leave his deck for treatment.

Promoted to Rear-Admiral in 1812 and honoured with a knighthood three years later, he died in 1830 in quiet retirement at his home in Marlow, on the Thames.

In the world of late eighteenth century American politics, Robert Morris is honoured in the historical record as one of the signatories on July 4, 1776 of the American Declaration of Independence and also on September 17, 1787 of the Constitution of the United States.

Born in Liverpool in 1734 and immigrating

to America when aged 13 to join his father who had established a business as a tobacco factor in Maryland, during the American Revolutionary War he was recognised as "the most powerful man in America" next to General George Washington.

Serving from 1781 to 1784 as Superintendent of Finance for the fledgling United States and also as Agent of Marine in charge of the navy, he served from 1785 until eleven years before his death in 1806 as one of the two senators for Pennsylvania.

The Robert Morris University in Illinois, Pennsylvania is named in his honour as as are a number of ships in the U.S. Navy and U.S. Coast Guard.

In British politics, John Morris, Baron Morris of Aberavon, is the retired Labour Member of Parliament (MP), who held a number of senior government posts.

Born in 1931 in Capel Bangor, Aberystwyth and studying law at the University College of Wales and at Gonville and Caius College, Cambridge he represented the Welsh constituency of Aberavon from 1959 until his retirement in 2001.

Secretary of State for Wales from 1974 to 1979, other posts he held included Parliamentary

Secretary to the Ministry of Power and the Ministry of Transport, Minister of State at the Ministry of Defence and, from 1997 to 1999, Attorney General for England and Wales and Northern Ireland.

Born in 1952, Estelle Morris, Baroness Morris of Yardley, is the former Labour MP who, in addition to representing the constituency of Birmingham Yardley from 1992 to 2005, served for a time in government posts that include Secretary of State for Education and Skills and Minister of Arts.

The daughter of Charles Morris, Labour MP from 1963 to 1983 for Manchester Openshaw and a niece of Alf Morris, Labour MP for Manchester Wythenshawe from 1964 to 1997, she was elevated to the Peerage of the United Kingdom as Baroness Morris of Yardley, of Yardley in the County of West Midlands, after stepping down from the government and as an MP at the 2005 General Election.

From politics to industry, John Morris was the leading British industrialist of the mid eighteenth to early nineteenth centuries who developed coal mining and copper smelting in Swansea, South Wales.

The enterprises had been started by his father

Robert Morris, the entrepreneur who first came to Swansea in 1724 to supervise the Llangyfelach Copper Works, taking over control of it in 1726.

John Morris expanded and developed the business to the extent that in 1768 he built the planned village of Morris Town, now known as Morriston, to house his workers.

Born in 1745, he died in 1819 after having been raised to the Peerage of the United Kingdom as a Baronet.

Not only a British motor manufacturer but also a noted philanthropist, William Richard Morris, 1st Viscount Nuffield, was born in 1877 in the Comer Gardens area of Worcester.

Moving with his family to Oxford at the age of three, he was apprenticed to a local bicycle-seller and repairer after leaving school when aged 15.

Less than a year later, aged 16, he was able to set up his own bicycle-repair business, run from the family home, later opening a shop in Oxford's High Street.

The business proved successful, and in 1901 Morris diversified into working with motorcycles, designing the Morris Motor Cycle and, in 1912, through further ambitious diversification, he designed a car, the Bullnose Morris and took over premises in Cowley, Oxford.

It was in 1928, after having taken over the bankrupt Wolseley Motors, that he launched his first highly successful and iconic Morris Minor.

He took over Riley (Coventry) in 1938, while in 1952 Morris Motors Limited merged with the Austin Motor Company to form the British Motor Corporation (BMC).

By 1968, BMC had merged with other British automobile manufacturers to become British Leyland.

Having been raised to the Peerage in 1934 as Baron Nuffield, he was further honoured three years later by being appointed Viscount Nuffield, of Nuffield in the County of Oxford.

In 1943, with an endowment of £10m, he founded the Nuffield Foundation to advance social welfare and education, while he also founded Nuffield College, Oxford.

He died in 1963, while his former home of Nuffield Place is now in the care of the National Trust.

In the arts, William Morris was the English textile designer, artist and writer born in 1834 in Walthamstow and who died in 1896.

Associated with the highly creative art movement known as the Pre-Raphaelite Brotherhood and the English Arts and Crafts Movement, he was also the author of famous fantasy novels that include his 1896 *The Well at the World's End*.

In the sciences, Elizabeth Morris, born in 1946, is the glaciologist who was head of the ice and climate division at the British Antarctic Survey from 1986 to 1999 and president from 2002 to 2005 of the International Glaciological Society.

A senior associate at the Scott Polar Research Institute, University of Cambridge, she is also the recipient of the Polar Medal for her services to Antarctic science.

In the highly complex realms of computer science, Robert Morris was the pioneering American cryptographer and computer scientist born in 1932 in Boston.

The recipient of a degree in mathematics from Harvard University in 1957 and a master's degree in applied mathematics a year later, he worked from 1960 to 1968 as a researcher at Bell Labs, playing a key role in the development of the computer operating systems *MULTICS* and then *UNIX*.

Serving later as chief scientist for the National

Security Agency's (NSA's) National Computer Security Center, before his death in 2011 he famously warned: "There are three golden rules to ensure computer security – do not own a computer, do not power it on and do not use it."

Rather ironically, it was his son the computer scientist Robert Tappan Morris, who was responsible in 1988 for creating the *Morris Worm*, the first computer worm on the Internet – with a 'worm' capable of exploiting a number of vulnerabilities to gain entry to targeted computer systems.

This was an act for which he was fined $10,050 and sentenced to 400 hours of community service and three years' probation.

Born in 1965, Morris had created the worm while a graduate student at Cornell University.

Rather more respectably, he now holds the prestigious post of a professor in the department of electrical engineering and computer science at the Massachusetts Institute of Technology (MIT).

Chapter four:

On the world stage

A former back-up dancer for the singer Beyoncé, Heather Morris is the American actress, dancer, singer and model best known for her role of the cheerleader Brittany S. Pierce in the highly popular television musical comedy series *Glee*.

Born in 1987 in Thousand Oaks, California and taking up dancing when aged nine, it was in 2007 that she was a dancer in Beyoncé's *The Beyoncé World Experience Tour*.

In addition to appearing in the television series of *Glee*, she also starred in the 2011 *Glee: The 3D Concert Movie*, while other big screen credits include the 2003, *Spring Breakers, the* 2008 *Bedtime Stories*, and the 2009 *Fired Up!*

Born in 1915, **Mary Morris** was the British actress who, after studying at the Royal Academy of Dramatic Art, London, made her stage debut in 1935 in a production of *Lysistrata* in the city's Gate Theatre.

Television credits before her death in 1988 include the 1967 series *The Prisoner*, *A for Andromeda* and *Doctor Who*, while big screen credits include *The Man from Morocco* and *The Face of Love*.

She was the daughter of the noted British botanist **Herbert Stanley Morris**, born in 1892, and who served as Britain's district commissioner on the island of Fiji and who was killed in an aircraft crash in 1919.

Back on the stage, **Sarah Morris**, born in Memphis in 1977, is the American actress known for her role of Julia Walker in the television series *Brothers and Sisters* and whose big screen credits include the 2000 *Coyote Ugly*, the 2008 *Seven Pounds* and, from 2012, *Willed to Kill*.

Born in 1937 in New Orleans, **Garrett Morris** is the American comedian and actor best known for his work from 1975 to 1980 in the comedy sketch programme *Saturday Night Live* – where he delivered impressions of celebrities ranging from Louis Armstrong and Muhammad Ali to Richard Pryor and Tina Turner.

An iconic figure of British television screens from the early 1960s until the early 1980s, **Johnny Morris** was the presenter born in Newport, Wales in 1916.

The son of a postmaster, it was while telling

stories in his local public house that he was talent-spotted by the BBC Home Service, making his radio debut in 1946 and going on to star in the popular zoology-based television programmes *Tales of the Riverbank* and, from 1962 to 1983, *Animal Magic*.

The recipient of an OBE and author of the autobiographical *There's Lovely*, he died in 1999.

Also in the zoological world, **Desmond Morris** is the English zoologist, ethnologist and painter born in 1928 in Purton, Wiltshire, who has authored a number of best-selling books that include his 1967 *The Naked Ape* and, from 1969, *The Human Zoo*, which was also adapted for television.

Bearers of the Morris name have also excelled in the highly competitive world of sport.

In the rough and tumble that is the game of rugby union, **Steve Morris**, born in 1896 in Newport, was the Welsh flanker who, in addition to earning 19 caps playing for his nation between 1920 and 1925, played for the amateur club Cross Keys.

Following the former coal miner's death in 1965, his ashes were scattered on the club's home ground of Pandy Park.

His contemporary namesake, **Steve Morris**, is the Australian former rugby league player born in

1957, who represented his nation in 1978 in addition to playing for clubs that include the St George Dragons and the Eastern Suburbs Roosters.

On the fields of European football, Arthur Grenville Morris, better known as **Grenville Morris**, was the Welsh inside forward who earned 21 caps playing for his nation between 1896 and 1912.

Born in 1877, before his death in 1959 he also played for clubs that include Aberystwyth Town, Swindon Town and Nottingham Forest.

From football to the cricket pitch, Samuel Morris, better known as **Sam Morris**, was the only person to date of West Indian heritage – apart from Andrew Symonds – to have represented Australia in Test cricket.

Born in Hobart in 1855 and having represented Australia in the Second Test of the 1884 to 1885 series against England, he died in 1931.

Also on the cricket pitch, **Russell Morris**, born in 1967 in St Asaph, is the Welsh former right-handed batsman and medium-paced bowler who played for the combined Oxford and Cambridge Universities side against New Zealand in 1990.

Born in London in 1914 of Irish roots, **Michael Morris**, 3rd Baron Killanin, was the journalist, soldier and keen sportsman who served from 1972 until 1980 as sixth president of the International Olympic Committee (IOC).

Also the author of a number of books that include his 1983 *My Olympic Years*, he died in 1999.

In the world of music, **Russell Morris** is the Australian singer and songwriter who has enjoyed international success with a number of best-selling singles that include his 1967 *Heat Wave*, the 1969 *The Real Thing* and, from 1992, *Stay with You*.

Born in 1948, he is also an inductee of the Australian Recording Industry Association (ARIA) Hall of Fame.

On American shores, **Paul Morris**, born in Santa Monica, California in 1959, is the rock keyboardist who has played and recorded with bands that include Richie Blackmore's Rainbow and The Teen Idols.

In the creative world of the written word, Christopher Crosby Morris, better known as **Chris Morris**, is the American author whose fiction and non-fiction work includes his 1988 *Tempus Unbound* and the 1995 *Weapons of Mass Protection*.

Born in 1946, he is the husband of fellow author **Janet Morris**, also born in 1946, and whose fantasy and science fiction works include her 1977 *The Golden Touch* and the 1982 *Earth Dreams*.

She has also co-written books with her husband, including their 1994 *The Stalk*.

Born in 1953 on the Wirral, near Liverpool, **Jim Morris** is the acclaimed English playwright of the genre known as social realism.

His plays include the 1981 *Blood on the Dole* – adapted in 1994 as a film for television.

One bearer of the proud name of Morris with a rather unusual claim to literary fame was the English Anglican priest the **Rev. John Morris** – who in 1950 founded the boys' comic *The Eagle*.

This was in response to his concern that imported American comics were having an 'unwholesome' effect on British children and he sought to provide something more 'uplifting.'

Also appointed editorial director in 1959 of the National Magazine Company and later as its editor-in chief, he was responsible for launching the British edition of the magazine *Cosmopolitan*.

Born in 1915 in Preston, Lancashire and the recipient of an OBE, he died in 1989.